Introduction to Stocks

How to Make Healthy Soups a

Cookery Series

Dueep J. Singh

Mendon Cottage Books

JD-Biz Publishing

Disclaimer

The information is this book is provided for informational purposes only. It is not intended to be used and medical advice or a substitute for proper medical treatment by a qualified health care provider. The information is believed to be accurate as presented based on research by the author.

The contents have not been evaluated by the U.S. Food and Drug Administration or any other Government or Health Organization and the contents in this book are not to be used to treat cure or prevent disease.

The author or publisher is not responsible for the use or safety of any diet, procedure or treatment mentioned in this book. The author or publisher is not responsible for errors or omissions that may exist.

Warning

The Book is for informational purposes only and before taking on any diet, treatment or medical procedure, it is recommended to consult with your primary health care provider.

Check out some of the other Healthy Gardening Series books at Amazon.com

Gardening Series on Amazon

Check out some of the other Health Learning Series books at Amazon.com

Health Learning Series on Amazon

Table of Contents

Introduction

Nobody knows when human beings began to make stocks and soups from meat and vegetables. This secret is lost in the mist of the ages. Stock is a liquid which is obtained when you boil vegetable or meat over heat for a long time.

This is going to contain some of the most important and soluble nutrients and flavoring constituents of the foods which have undergone the boiling process. These nutrients have been extracted by prolonged and gentle simmering.

Such a liquid is the foundation of soups, sauces and gravies in cuisines all over the world. The ancient Romans regarded a really good cook as a pearl beyond compare. Only he knew all about the herbs and spices which he was going to use in making a stock which would be then be used to make a gravy on which emperors would dine.

So is it a wonder that the first part of learning cookery is to know how to make a good stock.

The method of preparation is based upon the solvent action of the water and the prolonged application of moderate and moist heat. The gelatinous, lean and muscular tissue parts of the meat with a certain proportion of bone are most suitable to make the stock.

In ancient times, people who could not afford better cuts of meat, which went to the rich had to make do with the leftovers which were bones and pieces of lean meat. So it is natural that they tried to make these pieces very tasty by first boiling them in water. Then they added some herbs and some vegetables and then they added any available in gradient which could add to the rich flavor and aroma of something being cooked slowly on a fire.

Lo and behold, the first stock was made with the slow simmering of all these ingredients mixed together.

The importance of soup all over the world, especially in folklore cannot be disregarded. You may want to enjoy the traditional stories here about soup, from different parts of the world.

http://www.pitt.edu/~dash/type1548.html#stonesoup

Herbs and spices are not generally used for meat stock, nowadays though they were used in ancient times. Also, today they are added with discretion in fish and vegetable stocks, but like I said, in ancient times, everything went into the cooking pot and was stewed for a long time, before fed to a hungry family.

The vegetables should be fresh, not necessarily young and expensive and the trimmings and coarse stalks can be utilized. Ages ago, the food gatherer went hunting for roots, edible vegetables and other greens in the woods, and all of them were added to the cooking pot. Each portion of the plant including roots, shoots, and leaves, stems, flowers and bark if edible were utilized.

The vegetables generally used for making stock are carrots, onions, turnip and celery. Make sure that no flavor predominates. Turnip and celery, if it is old is particularly strong and should not be used in large quantities.

Vegetables are very absorbent of meaty flavors. That is why they should not remain too long in the stock while it is cooking. This is the same reason why cooks do not let them steep for long in the stock, after the stock has been removed from the fire.

Leaving the vegetables in the stock in hot weather is going to cause fermentation that is why in very hot weather and in temperate climates, traditional cooks never used vegetables in making stock.

What Goes in the Stockpot

Nowadays we just put all the stock ingredients in one huge saucepan, and allow to simmer on heat for a couple of hours. Some stocks are made for special purposes. However, general household stock was once always available as it was an everyday requirement in a household where food was needed at all hours of the day.

A large household was always full of members who needed something to eat at all hours and their hunger could be assuaged with some soup and some bread, until lunch or dinner time. Even though this is not the case, nowadays in many parts of the world, where we have small families, the tradition of making stock is not going to fade away into oblivion anytime soon.

A well-organized cooking should have a good household stockpot in which you can put odds and ends from the larder, scraps and trimmings from poultry and meat, cooked and uncooked pieces of meat, giblets and pieces of fresh vegetable as and when necessary.

Remember that everything should be perfectly fresh and free from the slightest suspicion of staleness. In olden times, when vegetables and meat was not so plentiful, they did not bother much about freshness and allowed the continuous stewing to get rid of the food poisoning causing bacteria, if any. Nevertheless, there were plenty of cases of food poisoning, with the cooked blamed everything except the ingredients in his stockpot .

The things which are not going to go into your stockpot are fatty items, cabbage, cooked vegetables, and any starchy materials such as thickened sauces, bread, etc., which are going to make your stock cloudy.

For a small family, the fireproof earthenware stockpot/Marmite which is glazed inside is excellent for making stock. This is going to be a non-absorbent thanks to the glaze. The lid prevents evaporation. It is also easy to clean and requires little fuel to keep the stock contents at simmering point.

In places where stock is made constantly and in a larger quantity, a metal stockpot with that and fitted inside with a strainer is very satisfactory. This is good enough for hotels

Absolute cleanliness of the utensil is essential, especially if it is used daily. You need to clean it meticulously after every use. Even a little bit of food sticking to the stockpot, and getting stale overnight can cause possible food poisoning.

How to Prevent Stock from Turning Sour

To prevent Stock from turning sour and this is very possible in hot weather, strain off the meat and vegetables as soon as the stock is removed from the heat.

The vegetables are of no further use being flavor less. So put them into your organic bin to be turned into compost. Or you may mash them and eat them yourself because none of the rest of the family is going to eat them.

When the stock is cold, remove the congealed fat from the surface. This stock has to be boiled again daily in hot weather and every second day in the winter.

The fat removed from the surface can be clarified and used for frying. After all it is concentrated fat. Surplus stock can be boiled down so that you can glaze roast dishes like roast meat with it.

How to Make Good Stock

There are plenty of modern methods in which you can make stock, but we are going by the ancient traditional method which has been followed down the centuries, where every bit of food is utilized economically.

Firstly, you need to see that the utensil is completely clean and the ingredients have to be fresh.

The bones and the meat have to be divided – butchers normally crack up the bones for you, especially when you tell them that you intend to use them for making stock – into manageable pieces. This is so that more surface area is exposed to the solvent action of the water.

You may want to steep the meat in cold water before putting on to the boil. Cold soft water is best because it has greater solvent action than hot and hard water.

The removal of white scum during the commencement and during cookery is necessary. This consists of impurities. However, do not remove the brown scum. This is coagulated protein matter. If you do not skim the stock, it is going to turn out cloudy.

If the vegetables are small, use them whole. If they are large, cut them up into large pieces. This is to prevent pulping, which is going to make the stock cloudy and to prevent the increase of the absorbent power of the vegetables.

Brown Stock

Brown Stock is normally made from shin bones, which have been cracked, so that you can see the marrow. For this you need 4 pounds shin of beef, four quarts of cold water, one teaspoonful of salt, carrots, onions, two stalks of celery or ¼ teaspoonful of celery seeds.

White the meat and remove any fat, cut into 1 inch cubes. Break bones, then remove marrow, if you are making a clear soup, marrow is going to make it cloudy

Cover the meat and bones with the water, add salt, and leave to steep for 30 minutes.

Bring slowly to boiling point and remove all the white scum.

After the stock has been boiling for about one hour, add the cleaned vegetables. Bring to a boiling point again, simmer gently for four – five hours skimming occasionally.

Strain through a sieve or a colander. This is to remove the bones in the vegetables. When it is cold remove the floating fat congealed on the surface.

White Stock

This is made as above with white meat, especially rabbit, poultry, knuckles of veal, and feet. The richest white stock is made from the knuckles of veal and poultry.

How to make A Meat Glaze

The glaze on the surface of the roasted meat adds to its attraction while serving.

Surplus stock can be made into glaze. For this, you need any good brown stock and the second boiling from the bones and the meat.

Remove every trace of fat, boil quickly with the lid on and skimming frequently. Reduce the liquid to about half a pint. Then reduce again, until it is about the consistency of treacle or syrup. Make sure that you keep stirring it continuously and well, because at this stage as it is going to burn readily.

If not required for immediate use, pour into a small jar, cover the surface with melted lard and cover tightly. Used for coating meat and for enriching sauces and gravy.

Making Perfect Soup

All the traditional culinary rules governing the making of soup is the same as those used in the making of stock. Soup is a liquid which contains the soluble constituents of its ingredients. You may thicken a soup or not as you wish.

Soup has long been an item of the daily diet of people all over the world for centuries. However, with the passing of time, it has become frequently neglected as an item in the daily diet. And that is why the general health of many people all down the generations has suffered because they have been deprived of this nourishing and health restoring nutrient. It should be eaten more generally for dietetic and economic reasons.

Warm food is more stimulating than cold food. That is why a soup is suitable, especially as a prelude to cold meat particularly in winter.

Hot soup is not only nourishing, but with extra ingredients added to it, like noodles and pieces of meat, this is a mainstay for your main course.

The utilized session of stock and of remnants of food, animal and vegetable with other additions are going to supply some of the necessary and essential nutrients needed to keep your meals healthy.

These would otherwise have been derived from meat, which is the most expensive form of protein. Not everybody can afford to eat meat every day. But vegetable soup, especially in which you have put some pieces of meat, a couple of days ago, can be cooked and reheated again can be used throughout the week.

Also, other foods which form tissue, and supply your body with heat and energy are going to be absorbed in your body, through the medium of soup. That is the reason why stimulating and nourishing soup is considered to be extremely important in invalid diets because it is easy to digest.

Soup Classifications

The foundation liquid which is used to make soup is either stock of various kinds or just water. Those soups, which are made without meat stock or meat are vegetable and fish soups.

You may classify soups as thin soups and thick soups.

Thin soups – These include clarified and clear soups, which you know as **consommé**. **Broths** are unclarified thin soups.

Beef consommé.

Thick soups include purees, a thickened soup which one calls a potage, brown soups, like oxtail and mulligatawny soup, white soups, including cream soups and bisques.

Food Value of Thick and Clear Soups

The value of soup as the food is going to depend upon the type. That means is the soup clear or is it a thick soup.

A clear soup, like a consommé is going to be prepared from first meat stock. First meat stock means either a white stock or a brown stock.

In the process of making such a stock, a portion of the meat constituents are extracted into the liquid. Some of the connective tissue is converted into gelatin.

Even a strong stock made with a very gelatinous meat is going to contain only a very low percentage of gelatin. But 1% of this product is enough to set the liquid.

A considerable quantity of mineral matter and nutrients, a small proportion of soluble proteins, and a small amount of fat are the other items which are going to be a part of the soup. The fat is removed by skimming.

The coagulated protein can also be removed by straining. It takes the form of the brown scum. But like I said before, remove the white scum and leave the brown scum, unless you are making a white soup.

The remaining liquid is going to have gelatin and all the extracted nutrients. This is your clear soup. This soup has little food value, but it is of extreme dietetic importance because it is an aid to digestion and a stimulant.

That is because it is chief constituents – nutrients and gelatins are going to promote the flow of the digestive juices.

For a soup to be nourishing as well as stimulating, it must be thickened either by the retention of its ingredients finely divided as in mutton broth, or sieved as in lentil soup. You can also thicken it by the addition of bulky healthy food items like macaroni, eggs, grated cheese, milk, and starchy food, especially cereals and their products.

On the other hand, thick soups are of considerable food value. In combination with other foods they are going to provide you with a major part of the nutrients necessary to make up a well-balanced meal.

In making soup, as with any other culinary process, a reliable basic recipe for a particular type of soup can be varied. That can be done when a budget conscious cook knows all about the food items at hand, and then nutritive value of each.

That is how she can provide her family with a considerable variety of nourishing household soups at a small cost.

Essentials of a Well-Prepared Soup

The first is of a well-prepared soup is, of course flavor. The flavor of a delicious, nutritious soup is always full and good. You can taste the chief and the foundation ingredients predominantly. Minor flavorings are going to be well blended. They should not be overpowering.

The major factors which are going to determine the perfect flavor of a soup are – **Perfectly Proportioned Ingredients** – this means that for every half a pound of meat, to 1 pint liquid, you need 1 pound of vegetables. If you are adding pulses to thicken the soup, you may want to add ¼ cups of pulses to every pint of liquid. 2 cups make a pint.

Quality of the stock – the ingredients have to be perfectly fresh and the stock also has to be fresh whatever its strength. Used first stock only for consommés and rich white soup

Steep the meat in cold water while you are cutting the ingredients.

Heat slowly to boiling point than heat gently and steadily simmer the soup to extract all the nutrients and flavoring constituents.

Use the vegetables, flavorings, herbs and spices judiciously. Over spicing is going to spoil the taste of the soup.

Seasoning – make sure that the seasoning is not in excess. A soup should not be required to be seasoned after it has been sent to the table. Salt should be added at the beginning of cooking.

No fat – make sure that the radiance which you are going to use in stock should be free from fat. Also, remove the fat from the soup meat.

The vegetables need to be sautéed carefully to ensure absorption of fat, if any.

Keep skimming at the beginning of the cooking after the boiling point has been reached. And then continue this skimming at intervals afterwards if necessary.

Consistency and smoothness – this refers to the thick soups only. The consistency should be like that of cream. It should not been thick like porridge, nor should it be as thin as milk. Consistency and smoothness is going to vary with the type of soup. A purée is going to be slightly thicker than ordinary thickened soup – a potage.

Vegetable purée.

Why Does the Consistency Vary?

The variation in consistency is due to a number of factors. Some of them are overlooked by cooks, but here they are –

Over reduction of liquid by too rapid cooking and by cooking in an uncovered pan means a thick consistency.

Insufficient cooking of ingredients and imperfect formation of the thickening which is also known as the liaison is another factor.

The smoothness of the soup is going to be affected by careless addition of any starchy ingredient, which causes lumps. It is also going to be caused by imperfect sieving and by not mixing the sieved portion thoroughly with the liquid.

Color

How to get the white color in a soup? For this you need a white lined pan and a wooden spoon. You also need to make sure that the vegetables are properly cleaned and trimmed. They should be kept in cold water until they are required. The vegetables should be white like potatoes, artichokes, and celery.

You do not add sautéed vegetables because this is going to color the mixture. For brown soups, you are going to use brown stock, and brown roux. Fried onions, especially cooked in bacon fat, improves the flavor and color of the soup.

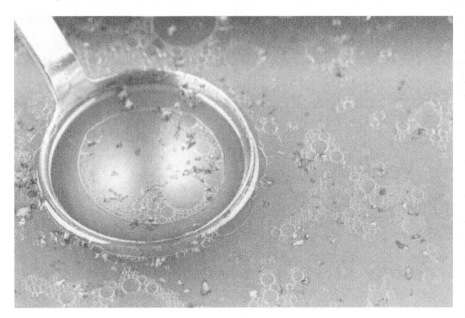

Liaison

This word is from the French word lier , which means to bind. That means that a thickening or abiding medium has been added to the soup, to give proper consistency and to ensure smoothness of texture. That binding agent has also been put in there to hold the ingredients together in suspension without which they would separate and settle at the bottom of the soup pot. This would happen when you are making lentil soup or tapioca soup.

Varieties of Liaison

The most popular **farinaceous agents** are flour, corn flour, arrowroot, tapioca, semolina and sago.

Roux is also used for binding. This consists of equal quantities of flour and fat.

Egg yolks especially when mixed with milk and cream are used for richer and more expensive white soups.

Tips When Using Liaisons

Thorough cooking is necessary when you have added a liaison. You do not want the taste of raw arrowroot or corn flour to seep through your soup, do you. Farinaceous matter is normally in powdered form. You have to mix this smoothly with a small amount of liquid. Then add this to the soup just before dishing and boil for at least five minutes, stirring the whole time.

 If you are using a small grain, such as semolina or crushed tapioca, this has to be cooked in the soup until it is quite transparent. This is going to take 15 to 20 minutes.

Roux

This is going to consist of equal quantities of fat and of flour blended over heat. It is going to be cooked for a sufficient time to color or not, as required.

To make the Roux you need to blend the flour smoothly with the fat, re-heat and cook slightly, being careful not to let it overheat and become oily. Do not allow it to color, especially if it is required for a white sauce or soup.

Draw the Roux away from the fire and add the liquid gradually, stirring it in gently. Otherwise, the soup is going to get lumpy. Boil again for another 7 to 10 minutes.

Overcooking a brown roux is very common, unless care is exercised. This overcooking causes the starchy matter to change and lose some of its thickening qualities and properties. This process causes the fat to separate, rising to the surface and the soup is going to become thin and greasy as a result.

Yolks of eggs mixed with stock, cream and milk are added to the soup just before it is dished. Sufficient heat is necessary to coagulate the egg albumen and to form the   liaison, but the soup should not be at boiling point when it is added or allowed to boil afterwards or the egg content will curdle.

Proportions of Ingredients for Liaison

¼ Ounces of flour to every one pint of liquid for purées made up of ingredients rich in starch like lentil purée.

Half an ounce of flour to 1 pint of liquid made the ingredients contain little starch, like tomato soup

Ordinarily, you are going to use ¼ ounces of cornflour

For the Roux you need 1 ounce of fat and one hours of flour to every one quart of liquid. One pint is 2 cups. One quart is 4 cups. One – two egg yolks to 1 pint of liquid and 4 tablespoons full of cream to 1 pint of liquid.

Consommé

A consommé or a clarified soup is a clear and bright liquid. It is prepared from first meat stock for obtaining a full flavor. This flavor is augmented by the addition of fresh vegetables and of meat juices.

The stock, which must be perfectly free of fat and sediment is cleared by the albumen of an egg white and meat. This rises to the surface scarring all the impurities with it. Sometimes a crushed eggshell is also put in the soup, acting as a filtering medium in a cloth through which the soup is strained.

One white of an egg and 4 ounces of lean beef is sufficient for one quart of stock.

Cloudiness is due to use of poor quality stock, especially stock that is greasy and has not been strained. Also, imperfect coagulation of the clearing agent causes cloudiness.

If you whisk the soup, after the boiling point is reached, the impurities are going to mix again with the liquid. That makes it cloudy. Also, not allowing the soup to settle before straining and lack of cleanliness of the pan or the straining cloth, especially if both are greasy, is going to destroy the clarity of the consommé.

Broth

I was rereading one of my favorite authors, Maurice Walsh, where one of his characters describes the young brave and smart Irish lad as a "broth of a boy". This accolade filled term shows how much value is put on a broth, which is a thin and unclarified soup. It is of very considerable food value much more than that of a consommé or clarified soup.

This is because it contains all the soluble constituents of its ingredients which include meat, vegetables and cereals. None of them are removed by straining and clearing.

Such a soup is both stimulating and nourishing and if it is made with an additional vegetables and cereal matter, and eaten with bread and potatoes, it is going to furnish a substantial dish in an economical two course meal.

Martin, wheel, beef, chicken, rabbit, and even sheep's heads can make excellent broth. You have to blanch the sheep head to clean it before using.

Blanching

This is a process of cooking, in which fruit, meat, or vegetables are plunged into water, which is boiling. They are then removed after a brief interval of time and then directly plunged into cold and iced water or run under cold water. This process is called "shocking" the food item to prevent the food from being cooked any further.

Traditional Mutton Broth

For this you need 1 pound of knuckle of mutton, 2 pints of cold water, one dessert teaspoonful of barley or Rice, one teaspoonful of chopped parsley, one small leek, one teacup full of mixed vegetables like carrots, turnips and onions, half a teaspoonful of salt, and pepper

Clean the meat, cut away from the bone, remove all the marrow from the bone and the skin and the fat away from the meat. Chop the meat into small, neat pieces.

Slice the leek if you are using it thinly. Also cut the vegetables into small pieces. Wash the rice and blanch the barley. This is necessary because otherwise the broth is going to be really cloudy

Put the meat, bones, and one teaspoonful of salt into the saucepan, bring slowly to boiling point and keep skimming over the surface occasionally.

Add the rice and the barley and simmer for 1 ½ hours. Add the vegetables and continue cooking for another one hour skimming occasionally.

Strain this through a fine sieve, and remove the bones and the fat from the surface of the broth.

Return the liquid and solid ingredients to the pan, add parsley, season to taste, and boil some more to remove the raw flavor of the parsley.

You can prepare chicken and veal broth in the same way, by using half a chicken to every 2 pints of water. You can also substitute sago, tapioca and arrowroot for rice and barley, especially if you are making this broth for invalid's diets. In that latter case, the omission of vegetables is often necessary because vegetables are hard to digest. The food value may be increased by a larger proportion of meat and by the addition of egg yolk just before serving.

Purées

Purées are most economical and easy to prepare of all the household thick soups. The liquid, which is stock, milk or water or a mixture of any two liquids is thickened by the retention of solid ingredients.

These items are first sautéed in fat to soften them, and to impart additional flavor and then by slow and thorough cooking, they are reduced to a pulp to a purée form. This is then sieved and mixed with the liquid.

To prevent the separation of the purée from the liquid, and to ensure the smoothness of the texture, by preventing a granular appearance and a proper consistency, you need to add a little bit of starchy matter. Normally, one teaspoonful of flour or cornflour to every one pint of liquid is sufficient, but the amount is going to vary with the quantity of starch already present in the pulped ingredients.

Fresh vegetables, fish, game, poultry, meat and pulses are largely used as purée foundations. These are accompanied with toasted bread. The addition of milk to these vegetablesPurées increase their food value,enriches the flavor and improves the color. Cream augments these qualities to an even greater degree.

Both the milk and the green should be added at the last. If it is boiled in the soup, the flavor is going to be altered and there is a tendency to curdle.

Vegetable Purées

These are normally made up of pulses, succulent vegetables like carrots, artichokes and potatoes and green and other vegetables of delicate flavor like spinach, asparagus, tomato and green peas.

Pulse purées

Hummus is a puree, served cold.

These are extremely popular in the East. These soups require slow and very thorough cooking. Otherwise they are going to have a raw and starchy flavor.

The time of preparation is going to vary with the kind of lentils used for cooking this soup

Lentils normally take one and a half hours, peas take two to 2 ½ hours and up to 3 hours or more, if the pulses are stale. That is because stale pulse is very difficult to soften.

The same method is also used for haricot beans, as for pea or lentil soup. But as this is a white soup, you omit the carrots.

Tie all the herbs, when used in a muslin cloth. A small hambone is an improvement to pulse soups and that is how it is normally made traditionally.

Salt must be added carefully, if you are using a liquid which has already been salted or the meat is salted.

Pea or Lentil Soup

This is a thick soup, and that is why a fog in London is normally called a pea souper – you cannot see through it.

For this you need half a pint of split peas, or lentils, 2 pints of cold water, ham or meat boiling or vegetable stock, one large onion, 4 – 6 ounces of carrots and turnips, two sticks of celery or ¼ teaspoonful of celery seeds, small bunches of herbs, 1 ounce of drippings, pepper and salt, one dessert spoonful of flour, half a pint of milk and toasted bread for serving.

Wash the pulses in cold water and soak overnight in the 2 pints of liquid which you are going to use. Strain off the liquid preserving it and slice the vegetables thinly.

Heat the fat in the saucepan and in the hot fat sauté the pulses, and the vegetables. Add the liquid, herbs and salt and bring to boiling point.

Skim and simmer until the pulse is tender, stirring occasionally. Now sieve and return to the pan, which has been rinsed

Mix the flour smoothly, with milk if it is used. If not, you can use a little stock or a little water. Stir this into the soup, boil for five minutes and season.

This is normally served with toasted or fried bread and in the case of pea soup, you can serve it with mint, which is a good digestive.

Thick Soups

A typical potage…

Thickened soups means that we are talking about the more expensive types of soups, brown and white soups, including cream type soups and potages. This is because of the number of liaisons which are added to thicken the soup and binding it.

These liaisons include cereals in granular form, such as rice and tapioca, added at the beginning of the cooking. The starch thickening the liquid is going to proceed as cooking continues.

Flour and cornflour are also mixed with a little liquid and add it to the soup shortly before dishing to make a white vegetable soup

Brown or white roux is added beforehand or after the ingredients are cooked in the liquid in hollandaise, oxtail and fish soups.

Egg yolk liaison mixed with cream or milk, in addition to a thickening of farinaceous matter is also added just at the last especially in cases of tapioca soup. This thickens slightly and enriches the soup as to food value and flavor.

Cream Soups

Tapioca Soup

For this you need 1 pint of good white stock, one teaspoonful of crushed tapioca, pepper, salt, for seasoning, half a cup of cream and half a cup of milk for liaison.

Put the stock in the white lined pan, because these are normally used for clear soups bring it to boiling point. Sprinkle the tapioca, simmer for 15 minutes until the tapioca is quite transparent.

Mix the egg yolks with the cream and the milk, strain into the soup, which must be well below boiling point. Otherwise the liquid will curdle. Or alternatively you can pour the hot soup gently and slowly onto the liaison mixture.

Re-heat slowly, but do not re-boil, until the egg thickens and the tapioca is suspended. Great care is necessary to make sure that curdling does not occur.

Season and serve.

Bisques

These are thickened soups, which are normally made with shellfish.

Lobster Bisque

For this you need one Lobster medium-size, 2 pints white stock, carrots, turnips, onions and celery, 4 – 6 ounces in a mix, bunches of herbs of your own preference, half a teaspoonful of anchovy essence, pepper, salt, lemon juice, 2 ounces of butter, 2 ounces of flour and two tablespoonfuls of cream.

Remove the meat from the lobster, chop that meat present in the claws into neat pieces and reserve for garnish. Wash the shell, which is about half a pound thoroughly and found with the butter and remainder of the lobster.

Place this in your pan, allow butter to dissolve before adding flour, fry slightly.

Add the stock, vegetables and herbs, bring to boiling point, skim and simmer for ¾ – 1 hour

Strain through a sieve and return to the rinsed saucepan, bringing to boiling point and skim.

Add the lobster meat, seasoning, few drops of lemon juice and anchovy essence. The cream should be added at the last. Serve with fried pieces of bread.

If you cannot afford lobster, it is more economical to substitute whiting. Two whitings are going to give you an equally tasty bisque without any vestiges of lobster shell.

There are a number of soups, which can either be thick or clear soups. Thick soups like mulligatawny, and tomato, as well as oxtail are sometimes cleared. To prepare them, make the stock with the ingredients given for one particular soup, but be careful to make any starchy ingredient do not brown either the meat or the vegetables.

When the stock is cold, and free from fat, strain and follow the directions given for clearing stock as instructed in the consommé section.

How to Sieve Soup Properly

You can use this process to sieve, not only soup, but any other mixture. Use 2 teaspoons for sieving. Stand the sieve with the narrow rim uppermost inside a basin. Pour a little of the soup or the mixture into the sieve. Rub it through with the back of the spoon. If necessary, moisturize the mixture with some of the liquid and with a clean spoon, remove what is on the underside of the sieve.

You can re-sieve the material collected on the underside. Mix the sieved and liquid portions well together before you reheat the soup.

Conclusion

I am sure this book has given you plenty of information on how to make different types of soups, especially when you are looking for healthy and nourishing meals for your family. So make sure that soup becomes an integral part of your daily diet right now.

In many parts of the world, a hearty meal always starts with the soup, but in this 21st century where we are not bothered much about healthy eating, we miss the soup course completely. We are thus depriving our body of essential liquids and nutrients, which would otherwise have helped keep our body strong and healthy.

Healthy eating is in your hands so start by adding soup to your culinary repertoire stop.

Author Bio

Dueep Jyot Singh is a Management and IT Professional who managed to gather Postgraduate qualifications in Management and English and Degrees in Science, French and Education while pursuing different enjoyable career options like being an hospital administrator, IT,SEO and HRD Database Manager/ trainer, movie , radio and TV scriptwriter, theatre artiste and public speaker, lecturer in French, Marketing and Advertising, ex-Editor of Hearts On Fire (now known as Solstice) Books Missouri USA, advice columnist and cartoonist, publisher and Aviation School trainer, ex- moderator on Medico.in, banker, student councilor ,travelogue writer … among other things!

One fine morning, she decided that she had enough of killing herself by Degrees and went back to her first love -- writing. It's more enjoyable! She already has 48 published academic and 14 fiction- in- different- genre books under her belt.

When she is not designing websites or making Graphic design illustrations for clients , she is browsing through old bookshops hunting for treasures, of which she has an enviable collection – including R.L. Stevenson, O.Henry, Dornford Yates, Maurice Walsh, De Maupassant, Victor Hugo, Sapper, C.N. Williamson, "Bartimeus" and the crown of her collection- Dickens "The Old Curiosity Shop," and so on… Just call her "Renaissance Woman") - collecting herbal remedies, acting like Universal Helping Hand/Agony Aunt, or escaping to her dear mountains for a bit of exploring, collecting herbs and plants and trekking.

Our books are available at
1. Amazon.com
2. Barnes and Noble
3. Itunes
4. Kobo
5. Smashwords
6. Google Play Books

Check out some of the other JD-Biz Publishing books
Gardening Series on Amazon

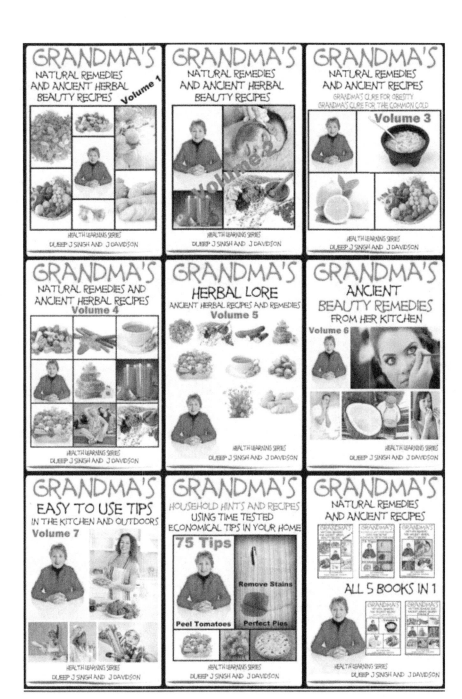

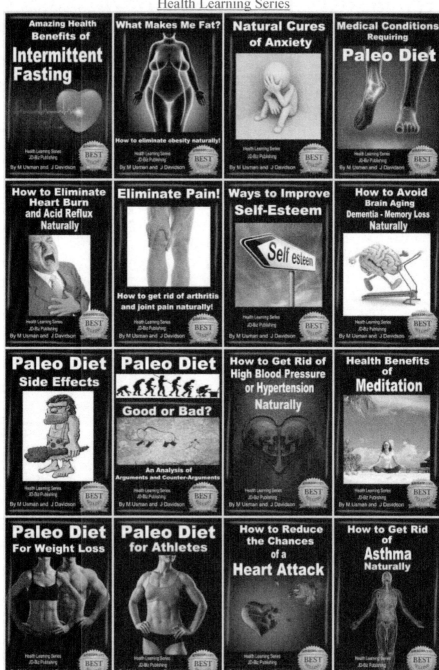

Amazing Animal Book Series

Learn To Draw Series

How to Build and Plan Books

Entrepreneur Book Series

Publisher

JD-Biz Corp

P O Box 374

Mendon, Utah 84325

http://www.jd-biz.com/

Printed in Great Britain
by Amazon